Elegy For The Undone.

Masoodi S.

BookLeaf Publishing
India | USA | UK

Made with ❤ on the BookLeaf Publishing Platform
www.bookleafpub.in
www.bookleafpub.com

Dedication

For the day this began

Preface

I used to believe poems were mirrors, an optics of the self, a technology of reflection in which the reader might locate her own image with sufficient clarity. I was wrong.
They were not mirrors. They were architectures. And I entered them without inquiring into their construction, their provenance, their intended inhabitants. I brought my questions with me and emerged with questions I did not recognize as my own.

Some poems held me. Some did not. Some produced the sensation of recognition. Others produced the sensation of standing at a threshold, illuminated but uninvited, a subject constituted by exclusion. I learned that beauty is not coextensive with belonging. That admiration can coexist with a kind of exile.

Still, I remained. Because something in me demanded reply.

These poems are not an attempt to revise what preceded them. They are the consequence of finding silence untenable. Because reading, if taken seriously, is not passive. It alters the reader. It shifts the ground beneath certainty. It undoes and remakes in the same breath.

If this is an elegy, it is just for loss. It is also for the moment of discovering oneself altered.

Perhaps you have known this too. The strange intimacy of being moved but not addressed.

This book begins there.

Acknowledgements

This book was written in conversation with people whom I have admired, resisted, misunderstood, and returned to. Even where I have taken exception, I remain in their debt. They altered me first.

To the writers who made language feel dangerous enough to matter.

To those who listened when these poems were uncertain and unfinished, thank you for your patience with my revisions, and with the silences between them.

To my family, who have witnessed the quieter transformations that do not make it into print.

And to the readers, especially those who have ever felt unaddressed. Thank you for stepping into these pages. This conversation is incomplete without you.

1. My Summer doesn't have a Sun

My summer doesn’t have a sun

I put the basket on the grass
like that would do something.
The fruit bled easy under the knife.
Napkins folded like dead birds.
The sky was that same blue
they paint on postcards.
Somebody said beautiful day.
Sure. Okay.
Laughter floated around like flies.
Touched my sleeve. Kept going.

My summer don't have a sun.

Up the trail behind them,
dust on my shoes.
The guide talking about rivers,
about places to rest.
I stopped for a rock in my shoe.
When I looked up and
nothing.
Just trees doing what trees do.

Light coming down in pieces
through the leaves.
I yelled something.
Came back wrong.
Like in somebody else's voice.

My summer don't have a sun.

They came back when it got dark.
Somebody said stick closer next time.
Somebody laughed too loud.
Fire going good.
I put my hands out and
felt nothing.
Just the idea of something.

My summer doesn't have a sun

Week later bought ice cream
from some guy with a broke bell.
Melted before I could pay.
Ran down my wrist.
Tasted like sugar and milk
Kid next to me lost his scoop,
started crying hard.
Real grief. Small and loud.
Mine just sat there.

Cold. Quiet. Precisely Mine.

My summer don't have a sun.

Somebody brought flowers.
Yellow. Trying hard.
I put them in water by the window.
Next morning they were dead.
Or close to it.
Water cloudy.
I waited for them to do something to me.
They didn't.

My summer don't have a sun.

Love came in like a contract.
I say this, you say that.
Quiet voices.
Like quiet fixes things.
Nothing spilled.
Nothing broke.
Just Nothing.

My summer don't have a sun.

Nights stay too long now.
Light on the wall won't leave.

I sit there
no shadow.
Season keeps going.
Fine. Perfect.
I'm still here.
Still Cold.

My summer don't have a sun.

2. Survival Mode

I wake up with my nails in my skin,
feet curled in,
arms tangled like they're holding up the house.
They ache all morning,
like they worked a shift I don't remember.

Little moons in my palms.
Nobody asks.
They're pretty. Almost.

Sometimes the air gets thick.
Tremor in my ribs
and I'm at the door
heart already in the street
looking for what broke.
Checking the buildings
And the cracks.

Nothing.
Just buildings.
Ground's fine.
Sky won't say shit.

I go back inside

carrying my shame
like skin I can't take off.

Jaw tight.
Teeth pressed together
like I'm keeping something in.
Even when I'm still
there's grinding.
A little factory
of pressure.

I sit in rooms where nothing is wrong
and then wait for the wrong thing to happen.
Tea gets cold.
Afternoons get dead.
Music plays
to nobody.

Don't enjoy much.
Not because the good stuff ain't there
but because it's gotta fight
through the noise.
But the noise always wins.

Maybe the world's fine.
Maybe the walls stay up.
But there's this hum

inside my head
all the time.
Low.
It Never stops.

The disaster outside
who knows.
The one inside
It never stops.

3. I will paint my nails blue

Maroon first.
looked like a scab that wouldn't heal.
i wore it on my hands
like something i'd earned.
thought if i went dark enough
i'd look like i meant something.

i didn't mean anything.
i was just red trying not to spill.

then blue.
told everybody it was for the sky.
never looked up long enough to know.
i wanted out.
called it depth.

then green.
bought plants. talked about growth.
they died one by one.
i didn't cry.
i threw them out.

then pink.
soft as a bruise that won't heal.

tried to be light in front of people.
it felt like smiling in a language i didn't speak.
i stopped.

then black.
black was easy.
black let me sit in rooms
and say nothing.
people left me alone.
i learned to like that.

then green again.
like a second try would change anything.
the new plants died too.
the dirt was always the same dirt.

then yellow.
thin yellow.
the color of cheap light.
i wore it like i was trying to convince someone.
maybe myself.
it didn't work.

color sits on top.
it never gets in.
you can paint the same wall forever.
underneath it's still the same wall.

i kept changing
like a woman trying on faces in a department store
mirror.
none of them fit.
none of them were hers.

I thought if i found the right shade
something would finally catch.
the paint never reaches the bone.

so.
I will paint my nails blue
sea blue.
the kind that doesn't answer.

And I will walk toward the water
hands at my sides.

step in and
the cold takes the blue first.
then the skin.
then the small warmth underneath
that i kept trying to prove was there.

4. Grief

To love life even
when it has bitten your tongue
and left the taste of iron there,
when the mirror gives back
a stranger
who wears a death mask
And your tired eyes.

When mornings arrive without invitation,
laying its pale palms on your face,
And you lie still as a nun in her stone bed
Wishing the light would pass over
Leave your room sealed
But it's bright hands force your eyes open

When the phone does not ring,
when the door does not open,
when the apology never comes
and the dead do not return
still, you put your feet to the cold floor

When grief loosens and tightens
like weather in your bones,

when memory sharpens its small knives
and calls it love,
let it sit
Sit at your table
Till it grows comfortable
And it's slow tongue learns the shape of your whole
body
Leaving it paralysed

And there will be days
when joy finally comes to you
Although it feels fraudulent,
like a dress borrowed from someone braver.
Wear it anyway.
Walk through rooms in its thin fabric
Stay cold in it

You will not always recognize
the person who survives you.
She will be quieter.
Heavier in certain places.
But there will be a steadiness
like a low flame that does not perform.

To love life is not to be dazzled by it.
It is no fairytale.
It is the act of returning

again and again
to the cracked cup,
the unremarkable sky,
the unremarkable breath.
the cold floor
the unrecognizable face.

5. Casket girl

I keep a box under the bed.
wood.
like a child's coffin but smaller.
for my size.
not for dying.
for the hours the skin doesn't fit.

some mornings i wake up almost right.
brush my teeth.
make myself breakfast.
the woman in the mirror nods.
we have an understanding.

then somebody looks at me wrong.
or doesn't look.
or looks too long.
the floor opens.

my chest fills with something black.
not water.
thicker.
old oil.
it climbs my throat.

love turns to teeth.
teeth turn to breaking.
i say things that crawl out of me
like roaches when the light hits.
later i find them in the corners of the room
and can't remember letting them out.

that's when i turn to the box.
I pull it from under the bed.
the wood is cold.
But it knows me.

I get in.
curled tight.
knees to chest.
In the dark i see them.
all the faces i wore like masks
before they cracked.
the woman i was yesterday.
the one last week.
the one who thought she was loved.
they stand at the door of the box
and watch.
they don't come in.
they never come in.

my heart beats like an animal in a cage.

it wants out.

hours pass.
maybe minutes.
time is a wound here.
it doesn't heal.
it just stops bleeding for a while.
when i'm in there
i don't have to love anybody.
don't have to be loved.
don't have to explain
why the smallest thing
breaks the biggest thing.

I just lie still
and wait
for the tide to pull back.
it always does.
eventually.

The box is the only thing that never leaves.
Some nights i lie on the floor
and slide my hand under the box
just to feel the wood.
just to know it's there.
just to know something's there.

and then i crawl out
and the world says
see?
you're fine.
you're normal.
you're okay.

i'm not fine.
i'm not normal.
i'm not okay.
i'm a woman with a box under her bed
and a face that falls off
and a chest full of black oil
and a heart that beats like a fist

6. Intrusive thoughts

my parents are speaking to me.
their mouths move like fish in a tank.
i am making frying custard.
the pan is hot.
the milk thickens on the burner.
cutting the banana
i chop my fingers instead.
the knife goes in like it always lived there.
blood clouds the yellow.
they eat it anyway.
they choke.
their faces go red then blue then still.
i watch from the stove.
the custard blackens in its pan.
i do not move.
i am a woman made of glass
watching through glass.

I take all the pills.
the whole bottle.
the white ones the blue ones the ones that keep me level.
i wash them down with tap water.
lie on the bathroom floor.
the tiles are cold and kind.

they hold me like a mother should.
i wait for the lights to go out.
they don't.
they never do.
the ceiling is a white eye
staring.

I let the gas on.
let it fill the kitchen like a slow breath.
then i light the match.
the house opens like a mouth.
the walls remember how to burn.
i stand in the yard and watch.
the tulips catch.
the curtains catch.
the bed where i never sleep catches.
i am cold and warm at once.
i am the match and the struck surface.
i am the house and the leaving it.

i pluck the only tulip that grew yesterday
in my garden.
it took weeks to push through the dirt.
i twist its neck.
it comes away easy.
the stem weeps clear water.

i put it in my mouth and chew.
it tastes like nothing.
like everything.
like the inside of my own palm.

i throw a glass bottle on someone.
a woman.
her head opens.
she looks surprised.
the blood is very red.
very red.
i walk past.
the glass crunches under my shoes.
i feel nothing.
i feel everything.
i feel nothing.

i bang my head to the wall.
the wall is older than me.
it does not give.
i do it again.
the sound is good.
a drum.
a heartbeat outside the body.
the plaster doesnt take my shape.
i press into it like a bed.

like a lover.
like a mother.

i electrocute myself enough not to die
but to get that rush.
the plug in my hand.
the current up the arm.
the arm locks.
the heart jumps.
for one second i am real.
for one second i am here.
then it stops.
then i am not.
then i try again.

someone crosses the road.
a man with a bag.
ordinary shoes.
hair that needs cutting.
i imagine
the car that doesn't stop.
the heart that stops instead.
the fall.
the knife.
the gas.
the match.

the pills.
the wall.
the wire.
the water.
the rope.
the drop.
the choke.
the bleed.
the burn.
the freeze.
the stop.

i count them on my fingers.
the fingers i cut instead of bananas.

my parents speak to me.
their mouths move like a fish in a tank
i pour the burnt custard down the sink.
it clots on the drain.
it looks like something that lived.
i leave it there.
i leave everything.
i am good at leaving.

7. Cage

Three mynas fell into my house
the way bad news folds into a morning
wrong place, wrong sky, wrong species of light.

They beat the windows open-mouthed.
Black rags against the invisible,
trying to finish a sentence
the glass had already erased.

Wing against what won't give.
Wing against what gives nothing.
The small arithmetic of things that can't get out

And my first thought was the old one:
let them die.

Not because I'm cruel
Because I know the shape of what I'm watching.

I have spent twenty five years hitting windows
I have left my feathers in every locked room.

A body dropped into a house
where the sky is just paint on the ceiling,

where every direction is a wall
wearing a disguise

They hit the glass again,
again,
again

like freedom was a woman
who might finally notice
if you just keep bleeding.

I thought about people.
How we grow into our cages.
How the lungs forget there was ever anything but this
air.

Give it time, I thought.
They'll learn the corners like prayers.
They'll eat from the floor.
They'll stop looking up.

The house is patient.
It has buried better things than birds.
It has buried me piece by piece as i kept bleeding.

the birds didn't learn the lesson.

They kept throwing themselves
at the light.

One window to another,
another,
another

small dark things against the clear face of God
who was not home.

And I watched them
with a mouth full of splinters:

some things would rather
empty themselves against the world

than fill themselves
with the world's small air.

I opened the door.
They couldn't see it.
Too busy dying toward the wrong kind of sky.

I know that blindness.

8. Butterflies

The scented candles are obedient
animals
they burn quietly,
Vanilla on the air
like perfume on a corpse.

On the table
A knife sleeps in its narrow spine of
metal.
It does not lie.
It has never lied.
It knows exactly where the skin stops
and the rest begins.

I pick it up.
Put it down.
Pick it up.

The bottle watches.
Empty thing.
Thing that once held something.
Thing that remembers holding.

I put my mouth to its mouth.

Nothing comes out.
Nothing ever comes out.

Inside me the butterflies
have stopped knocking.
They float now.
Little winged casualties
of a war I started
and cannot name.

The candles gutter.
The knife shines.
The bottle fills with shadow.

I open the knife.
It yawns.
It has been waiting all evening
to be useful.

I run my thumb along its edge
the way some people pray.
Blood rises in a thin red line.
It does not hurt.
Nothing hurts anymore.
The nerves learned to look away.

I watch the blood bead

like tiny eggs
laid under the skin.
I want to hatch them.
I want to see what comes out.

The bottle watches.
Its throat is dark.
I think about swallowing it.
Not the contents.
The glass itself.
How it would feel going down.
How it would cut from the inside.
How I would finally be
what I have always been
a thing that breaks
and keeps breaking.

The candles have burned low.
The vanilla is sick now.
Sweet and rotten.
Like a child's birthday
held in a hospital.

I remember being small.
I remember learning
that love has teeth.
That hands that hold you

can also hold you under.
That the softest voices
sometimes say the hardest things.

The knife remembers too.
It does not forget.
It does not forgive.
It only waits.

I press it to my wrist.
Not to cut.
Just to feel the cold.
Just to know it is there.
Just to practice.

The bottle fills with my reflection.
I do not recognize the face.
It looks like someone
who has been dead for years
and forgot to stop moving.

I put the knife down.
I pick it up.
I put it down.
This is a dance.
This is the only dance I know.

The butterflies have sunk lower.
They rest at the bottom of me.
Their dead eyes open.
They saw this coming.
They always see it coming.

I want to tell someone
but there is no one.
There is only the knife
and the bottle
and the dying candles
and the vanilla
that keeps breathing
like a thing that does not understand
it is already burning.

I am the thing that does not understand.
I am already burning.

I take the knife to my arm.
Not deep.
Just a line.
Just a sentence
the skin has been trying to write
for years.

It opens like a mouth.

It speaks in red.
It says what I cannot.

The bottle watches.
It has no mouth.
It has never spoken.
It understands.

I make another line.
Another sentence.
A paragraph.
A page.

The skin is patient.
It takes dictation.
It does not interrupt.

The candles die.
One by one.
The vanilla chokes
and stops.

Remains the knife
and the bottle
and me.

I cannot see the cuts

but I feel them.
Little mouths
breathing night air.
Little mouths
finally saying something true.

The bottle glints.
I reach for it.
I hold it by the throat.
I bring it close.

In the dark
I cannot tell
where the bottle ends
and I begin.

We are both empty.
We are both waiting
for something to pour in
that will not come.

I press the bottle to my chest.
It is cold.
It is the coldest thing
that has touched me
all week.

I think about my mother.
I think about how she held me
like this.
Cold.
Distant.
Full of nothing I could drink.

The knife waits on the floor.
It has done its work.
It is satisfied.

I am not satisfied.
I am never satisfied.

I feel for the cuts.
Wet lines.
A map of somewhere
I have never been
but keep visiting.

I press into one.
It opens wider.
Obliging thing.
It knows its purpose.

The bottle rolls away.
I hear it hit the wall.

It does not break.
Nothing breaks.
Nothing ever breaks the way you want it to.

I lie on the floor.
The cuts breathe.
They are the only living things
in this room now.

The candles are cold.
The knife is patient.
The bottle is somewhere in the dark
being empty.

I am somewhere in the dark
being empty.

We keep each other company.
We do not speak.
There is nothing to say
that the skin has not already written.

Tomorrow I will wake.
The cuts will be tighter.
The blood will be brown.
The knife will be where I left it.

Tomorrow I will pretend
this did not happen.

I put my hand over my mouth.
I press.
I press until I cannot breathe.
This is also a kind of truth.

The hand does not move.
It is my hand.
It is not my hand.
It belongs to someone
who wants me quiet.

I let it stay.
I let it press.
I let it have its way.

This is how it has always been.
This is how it will always be.

The butterflies have no opinion.
They are dead.
They are done.

9. The hunger

They said I was not starving.
Look at the gilded plate they shoved beneath your chin.

They stuffed my ears with wool and verbs,
crammed my mouth with the soft white bread of
obedience,
laid books upon my tongue like wafers,
and strung my neck with coins, heavy, cold,
each one a medal for a war I never won.

When the dark thing in my chest began to mourn,
a low sound behind the ribs,
they did not touch it. They did not even look.
They simply opened a leather purse
and threw their currency onto the wound.
It did not heal. It only rang,
a small, metallic bruise against the floor.
Buy yourself a window,they said.
Buy a new mouth.

So I ate. God, how I ate.
I swallowed the discipline. I devoured the degrees.
I gorged on rooms with polished, empty views,
on a future they had folded for me,

sharp and white as a hospital sheet.
I packed it in, all of it, until my belly was a drum
of tight, accomplished skin.

But something else was feeding.
A feral thing with hollow ribs and wire teeth,
it turned inward and began to gnaw.
It was dining on the meat of my own back,
sucking the marrow from my bones,
because the hunger was never for their bread.

It was never for the bright, false coin of comfort.
It was for a hand.
For a voice that did not weigh its words for worth.
For someone to cup the trembling, hairless creature
living in my chest, and without counting,
without flinching, press it to the furnace of their own heart
and let it feed on that.

Instead, they tallied me.
Instead, they paid the asking price and left me
on the counter, a satisfied transaction.

And I stand here, in the perfect, silent kitchen,
my pockets dragging the floor with gold,
a well-fed ghost,

while the animal in my chest, the real one,
finally, quietly,
gnaws on the silence I have become.
They said I was not starving.
So they fed me to myself.

First, they peeled the skin of want
and found it empty.
Beneath, the muscles of my longing
were neatly catalogued, weighed on scales,
pronounced sufficient.

Then they opened the cage of my chest.
The animal inside had stopped its keening.
It had grown quiet, professional,
and was now engaged
in the careful work of excavation
hollowing out the chambers of my heart
with the small, precise tools
they had given me instead of hands.

Look, they said, pointing to the cavity.
There is plenty of room in there.
Plenty of space for more achievement.
They poured another bag of coins
directly into the wound.
They did not notice the animal

had begun to eat its own tail,
a perfect, self-sustaining circle of consumption.

When they pulled back the lips of my mouth
to inspect my teeth,
they found only the ground-down stumps
of every word I had swallowed.
They marveled at the architecture of my jaw,
how it had been wired shut so elegantly
with gold thread and expectation.

They removed my eyes for examination.
Polished them with the soft cloth of their concern.
Placed them back in their sockets backwards
so that forever I would see only the inside of my own skull
the dark, the wet machinery.

They sewed me up with currency,
each stitch a transaction,
a small, glittering scar that would never close.

And still they insisted I was full.

But at night, when the counting stopped,
I would lie in my polished room

and feel the animal stir.
It had finished with my bones.
It had licked the marrow clean.
Now it was pressing against the walls of me,
sniffing at the seams they had sewn,
hungry for the only thing left:

to be let out.
To show them what their feeding had made.
To wear my skin like a coat
and walk, finally, on two legs
into their warm, well-lit houses
with nothing in its mouth
but the silence I had become
and the sudden, terrible need
to fill them up
with the dark.

Now I am standing at the mirror
and my reflection is gnawing on itself.
It has learned to multiply.
There are dozens of me now,
each one smaller, each one hollow,
each one holding out a hand
that is not a hand
but a receipt.

I try to scream
but the sound that comes out
is the clink of small indifferent bells.
I try to weep
but my eyes have been priced and sold.
I try to die
but the animal inside me
has already died for me
and left me here
a well-fed monument
pockets full.
belly full.
mouth full.
still hungry.

10. Cold

I have become a winter that does not end.
Not the kind that dusts the pines for postcards,
but the kind that gets into the marrow
and crystallizes there.
The kind that kills the garden
not with one hard frost
but root by root
until the ground remembers nothing
but the shape of cold.

They come anyway.
They always come.
With their small lantern faces.
Come out, they say.
Come back to the warm.
They bring soup in jars.
They bring their new babies.
They bring the ordinary light
that falls on tables
where people still remember
how to feel.

And I stand at the window
watching them knock.

Something in my throat
has calcified.
I am the one with the feet turned backward
So every step i take
Leads further from the world
They keep telling stories about me
But I was just a woman
Who once loved
And was maybe loved back
And in my own wretched imagination
In my paranoia
Loving stopped
And something in my feet remembered only
how to leave

Trauma has done this.
It has made me a bride
with no mouth for the wedding.
It has made me a door
that only opens inward
onto rooms so cold
even ghosts
choose other houses.

So I say no.
No to the soup.
No to the baby.

No to the simple hour
that asks nothing
except that I sit
in the same warm room
with the living
and pretend
I am still one of them.

I watch their faces close
like curtains.
They leave slowly,
careful not to startle
the quiet I have trained
to guard the door.

The house remembers though
The walls grow teeth.
The empty chairs
fill with the ones I failed
not the dead,
but the living I refused.
The birthdays I did not attend.
The hands I did not hold.
The laughter I let shatter
mid-air
like glass
dropped on a frozen pond.

They sit in my kitchen.
They drink my air.
They are the only company
I know how to keep.

I walk through the house
touching things.
The cold floor
The locked door.
I press my palm
to the window.
The glass drinks my heat.
On the other side
my reflection stares back
the woman in the tale
who was deemed inauspicious
by the priest
because her face
was too beautiful
or not beautiful enough
or because the stars
aligned against her
on the day she was born.
They sent her back
to her parents.
She walked alone

through the snow
and no one
opened the door.

In the kitchen
the tea they brought
has grown a skin.
I drink it anyway.
It tastes like the river Lethe
the one that makes you forget.
I have been drinking it for years.
I have forgotten everything.
How to warm.
How to want.
How to open a door
without first calculating
how much it will cost
to close it again.

Outside the snow
keeps falling.
It covers the garden
where nothing grows.
It covers the door
I will not open.
It covers the footprints
of everyone who tried

and everyone who will.

I am the Snow Queen
in her palace of ice,
sitting on a throne
made from every hand
she refused to take.
I have become a winter
that does not end.

I have become a person
who locked their own door
and then spent decades
pressing their ear to it
listening for footsteps
that will never come
because I taught them
not to.

And somewhere
in the frozen yard
beneath the snow
that never melts
the key lies buried.

I know exactly where it is.
I put it there.

I remember.

My hands
have forgotten
how to dig.

11. Panic room

It comes like a hand from inside.
Like something waking up that should have stayed asleep.

The heart stops being heart
It becomes fist
Fist punching ribs from inside

The lungs close.
Not slowly.
Not like holding breath.
You suck air but air says no
Like someone put a fist through the wall of the chest and grabbed your lungs
And squeezed them

You stand up.
You don't know why.
The legs are moving.
The legs are screaming RUN
You are already running inside yourself
You hit the wall.
You didn't see the wall.
The wall is there.

The wall has always been there.
But now the wall is the only thing between you and nothing.
You press your back against it.
The cold is good.
The cold is real.
The cold is the only real thing left.

The room is breathing.
The walls are breathing.
They pull in. They push out.
They are alive.
They are alive and they are hungry.

The floor tilts.
Not like a boat.
Like a mouth opening.
Like something below wants you to fall in.
Wants to swallow you down into the dark
Where the dirt is
and the dead things are

Your skin is wrong.
It's too tight.
It's too small.
You are a animal grown too big for its fur.
You want to tear it off.

You want to peel yourself down to the bone
just to breathe.

The hands are not hands.
They are things.
Crawling things.
They shake like leaves in a storm
The skin sweats ice
The stomach drops away like an elevator with cut cables
You are dying
This is what dying must feel like

You look at the door.
The door is ten miles away.
The door is in another country.
You will never reach it.
You will die here.
On this floor.
Against this wall.

The dark creeps in at the edges of the eyes.
Not sleep.
Not passing out.
Something else.
Something that wants to pull you under.
Something that wants to keep you.

You fight it.
You don't know why.
There's no reason to fight.
The thing has already won.
But you fight anyway.
Because that's what the animal does.
The animal fights until the teeth close.

And then.
Like a bad dream losing interest.
It lets go.
You slide down the wall.
You sit on the floor.
You are wet.
You are empty.
You are something that was almost taken.

And you know.
You know with a cold that never leaves:
It's still in there.
The thing.
It's sleeping now.
But it's in there.
And it knows where you live.
And it knows how to find you.
And it always.

Always.

Comes back.

12. The second skin

They were all so good at curtains.
My mother, she could draw them shut
with a word. Hush, she'd say,
as if I'd spoken out of turn.
These things happen. Like chicken pox.
Everyone gets it. You just don't talk about the spots.
She smoothed my hair
with the same hand she used to fold sheets.
I was just another crease to flatten.

My brother's mouth went small and mean.
"Eleven years you waited?
Eleven years to drop this
on the living room floor?"
He kicked at the air near my confession.
"Some things, you keep them.
You put them in a box.
You don't take them out
and make everyone look."
He looked at me
like I'd brought mud inside.

My father became a window
with the blinds pulled down.

I could see his shape behind the glass,
moving through his day,
but his face was always
turned away. Once,
I caught his eye
and saw nothing there.
Not anger. Not shame.
Just a man practicing
how to be empty.

My sister nodded.
She nodded for months.
"I'll call", she said.
"I'll come get you."
Her voice was a hand
reaching across water.
But the water kept widening.
She became a shore
I could see but never touch.
She had a life to live.
She lived it.
Away from me.

And I learned
that the worst part
isn't what happened
in the dark.

It's what they did
in the light.

They taught me
that my body
was a story
no one wanted to read.
That my pain
was a guest
who arrived too late
for dinner.
That my voice
was a radio station
they could simply
turn off.

So I turned it off myself.
I became what they wanted:
a girl with a painted smile,
a girl with weather inside her,
a girl whose mouth remembered silence.
I walked through rooms
like a ghost practicing
for her own death.

But at night,
my body remembers everything.

It remembers the weight.
It remembers their weightlessness,
how light they became
when my suffering
required them to be heavy.

It remembers my mother's sponge
soaking up my words.
My brother's keys
locking my history in a drawer.
My father's blindness,
that expert blindness,
practiced daily until perfect.
My sister's footsteps
fading, fading, fading
until they were never here at all.

And I lie awake
and feel the betrayal
like a second skin,
grown over the first.
Not just what was done ,
but what wasn't done after.
The bodies that walked past
the hurt,
and called it a rug,
called it a shadow,

called it a girl who should learn
to keep her own house clean.

They said if I pretend it's not there, it's not.
So I pretended.
I pretended so hard
I forgot where I ended
and the lie began.

Now I am a room
with a stain that keeps spreading.
And everyone who could have helped
has moved out of the house.
And I am left here,
holding the sponge,
wringing it out
over and over,
watching the same water
fall on the same floor.

It was not the monster in the closet.
It was the people outside the door
who heard me knocking
and decided
I was knocking wrong.

They taught me how to stay broken.

They handed me the pieces
and said,
"Look what you dropped.
Look what you did.
Look what you are."

And I looked.
God help me, I looked
until their faces
were the only mirror
I had left.

13. The Spider Philosopher

In the corner of my ceiling
a spider has been thinking.
All morning
she walks the thin geometry of her web
like someone waiting
for a door to open.
The web trembles.
If a fly never arrives
was the web still worth building?
If the wind destroys it tonight
does that make today meaningless?
She waits.
Eight legs folded
like the years I folded myself
into smaller and smaller rooms.
I watch her from my bed.
She builds.
Something tears it down.
She builds again.
No speeches.
No complaints.
Just silk
thinner than breath
stretching across

empty air.
Perhaps this is her philosophy:
that life
is the quiet courage
of making fragile things
again
and again
and again.

But here is what I know
that she doesn't:
The flies stopped coming
years ago.
She builds for a world
that has forgotten
how to be caught.
I want to tell her
to stop.
Rest your eight tired legs.
Let the dust take you.
Let the silence win.

She falls sometimes.
Drops from the ceiling
on a thread
thin as the reason
I kept going.

She hangs there
spinning
slowly.

If you've never hung like that
you don't know
how long a body can dangle
over nothing
and still call itself alive.

I am her child.
She is mine.
We build
in corners
no one cleans.
We build
knowing
the broom comes.
We build
because the alternative
is becoming
the dust.

And when the web breaks
and she falls
and climbs
and breaks

and falls
and climbs
I think:

this is what they made of me.
A creature
who builds her own
destruction
into the blueprint.
Who calls the falling
practice.
Who calls the climbing
hope.
It's not hope.
It's just legs
that keep moving
because stopping
would mean
admitting
that no one
is ever coming.

The spider
has become
a philosopher.

She says:

pain is just silk
you haven't woven yet.

She says:
the broom is not personal.
It's just a thing
that moves
through the world.
She says:
you can spend your life
wondering why
the wind destroys
what you make
or you can spend your life
making.
She says this
with no mouth.
She teaches this
with no students.
She believes this
with no faith.

I watch her
from my bed
where I am still learning
to be a girl
who was broken.

Perhaps this is her philosophy:
that life
is the quiet courage
of making fragile things
for no one
to see
again
and again
and again
until one day
you realize
you aren't making
for anyone anymore.

You're making
because the silk
is there.
Because the legs
still move.
Because the corner
is still yours.
Because somewhere
in the vast indifferent room
a girl is watching
and the watching
is a kind of building too.

And when I finally sleep
I dream
that I am the spider
and the spider is me
and we are hanging
from a thread
so thin
And below us
nothing.
No one.
Above us
nothing.
Just ceiling.
So we hold on.
We hold on.

14.

15. Occupation

The body is Gaza.
Not the news.
Not the numbers.
Not their graphs of the dead.
The body.
My body.
This body.

She controls the borders.
Not the crossings—the borders.
Every pore is a checkpoint.
Every breath must be processed.
Nothing enters without her stamp.
Not bread.
Not medicine.
Not the names of the dead who are still dying inside me.
I wake hollow.
She has counted the calories of grief
and decided hunger is a privilege.
She says the siege keeps us safe.
Safe from what?
Safe from whom?
She does not answer.
She is the answer.

She lives in the skull.
Not like a thought—like a garrison.
She has floodlights in the sockets.
She scans the horizon of the frontal lobe
for anything that looks like tomorrow.
Hope is a bullet.
She finds it every time.
She shoots it through the soft palate.
It lands somewhere in the throat
and stays there,
lead,
undigestible,
permanent.

Outside, the sea is visible.
I can see it from the window of the left eye.
Blue.
Open.
Moving.
Free.
I lick the glass for salt.
I press the forehead to the pane
until the skin remembers what water feels like.
She comes up behind me—no,
she is already there,
she is always already there

and pulls the curtain.
She says the sea is dangerous.
She says the fishermen are hiding something.
She says look away.
She tapes my eyelids open
and makes me watch the flashes of my wretched past.

She has taken the electricity.
Not the wires—the light.
The lights flicker like dying things.
They go out for hours.
For days.
For years.
In the dark,
I feel her moving through the organs,
like a census taker,
counting my lungs like ammunition,
weighing my liver like spoils,
deciding which part of me
will be donated to the occupation.
She is thorough.
She is always thorough.
She has clipboards in the blood.

She bombs the hands at dawn.
Not with sound—with silence.
I wake to find them useless,

numb,
curled like burnt things,
like the hands of a girl
who reached for something once
and was told to stop reaching.
She says it was necessary.
She says they were throwing stones.
She says the stones could have been weapons.
What stones?
I ask.
What hands?
She does not answer.

The lungs are under shelling.
Not with metal—with memory.
Each breath is a building collapsing inward.
I inhale the dust of the house I was born in.
I exhale the ashes of the grief
She watches from the ribcage,
perched on a sternum like a sniper,
taking notes,
adjusting the range,
firing again.
Breathe, she says.
Just breathe.
As if breathing were not the problem.
As if breathing were not the war.

She has blocked the water.
Not the pipes—the throat.
The throat is dry for weeks.
For months.
For the whole of my twenties.
I beg for one word,
one swallow,
one syllable of relief.
She offers salt.
She calls it rain.
She offers ash.
She calls it bread.
She says there is a shortage.
She says I should be grateful for anything.
She says this is how love works.

She has divided the body into zones.
The north: the eyes, still watching but not believing.
The south: the feet, still trying but not moving.
Between them, the checkpoints.
The heart cannot cross.
The heart is a sealed border.
She renews the permits slowly.
She enjoys the waiting.
She enjoys the watching.
She enjoys.

The schools inside the body are closed.
Not the buildings—the memory.
The memory of my mother's face
is being revised.
They are removing the softness.
They are adding barbed wire.
The history of my father's name
is being erased entirely.
It never existed, she says.
You never existed, she means.
She is rewriting the curriculum
in the soft tissue of the thighs,
in the scar tissue of the wrists.
She calls it peace.
She calls it peace until the word means nothing,
until peace is just another word for this,
for her,
for the slow erasure of everything that breathed.

In the morning,
she allows a ceasefire.
She opens the borders for an hour.
I rush to the throat
to swallow something wet.
There is nothing.
I rush to the hands

to see if they remember how to hold.
They do not.
I rush to the heart
to count the living.
There is only me.
There is only me and her
and she is me
and I am her
and we are the war
and I do not know anymore
where I end
and she begins
or if there was ever a beginning
or if there was ever an end
or if there was ever a me
that was not also her.

She shows me the plans
Plans to ruin what is left of me
She asks for my input.
She waits.
She enjoys the waiting.
She enjoys the asking.
She enjoys the knowing that I know
and the knowing that I cannot stop her
and the knowing that I will help her
because helping her is how I survive

and surviving is how I lose
and losing is how I stay alive
enough to lose again tomorrow.
She calls it peace

And I—
I am the child still digging.
I am the child always digging.
In the dark of the chest,
in the rubble of the lungs,
in the ruins of the throat,
I dig with what is left of the nails,
with what is left of the teeth,
with what is left of the voice
that was never allowed to speak.
I am looking for something.
A pulse.
A vein.
A single unbroken capillary.
A name.
A name she forgot to erase.
A name that has not yet been translated
into their alphabet.
A name that still sounds like home.

She does not hear.
She does not hear the digging.

She does not feel the passage
being carved behind the liver,
under the tongue,
through the soft, forgotten places
she stopped watching years ago.
She does not know
that the occupied
are always tunneling.
She does not know
that the dead
are always rising.
She does not know
that the child
is always growing
teeth in the dark.

16. Love

I stood at the window of my own face
and watched them.
They were making plans for happiness.
Small plans.
The kind that fit in teacups.
The kind that fold into drawers
with the lavender and the linen.
I was not among them.
I have never been among them.

the evening has arranged itself politely.
The way evenings do
pretending not to notice the wreckage.
Inside my head, the sirens had already begun.
They began in my childhood
And became my second religion.

Yet I opened the door to love.
Yes, I opened it.
Again and again I opened it.
I opened it like a wound
that has never stopped bleeding.
I opened it like a mouth
that has never stopped screaming

but learned to scream
only inside.

But something in me
not something.
Someone.
The one who lives in the skull.
The one who counts the exits.
The one who learned,
in the small room,
that love is a trick,
that hands are not for holding,
that kindness is the preface
to the thing that comes after—
kept asking for proof.

Proof of the tone in your voice.
Proof of the direction of your eyes.
Proof of the pauses between your words.
I needed to know
where the danger hid.
I needed to find it
before it found me.
I needed to be the one
holding the knife
for once.

Explain this breath.
Explain that glance.
Explain why silence fell between us
like dust on unused furniture,
like snow on a fresh grave,
like the weight
that still presses certain hours
flat as pressed flowers,
flat as the child
who learned to lie still
and wait for it to end.

My paranoia sat with us at the table.
Not a guest.
Not a shadow.
A third person.
It drank from your cup.
It studied your hands
as if they were maps
hiding the road to the small room.
It watched your mouth
for the lie I knew was coming
because all mouths lie,
because all hands take,
because all love
is just the preface.

You spoke gently at first.
You spoke gently for months.
For years.

No, nothing is wrong.
No, I meant nothing by it.
My intentions are not wrong.
No, I am still here.
Yes, I love you.
Yes, only you.
Yes, always.

But the questions multiplied.
They bred in the dark.
They had teeth.

Where were you?
Who were you with?
Why did you smile?
Why did you pause before answering?
Why did you look away?
Why do you love me?
Why?
Why?
Why?

The whys piled up

like bodies.
Like the bodies I carry
behind the ribs.
Like the child I buried
in the basement of the spine
who still screams
but only at night
and only inside.

Even the quiet had to be explained
Especially the quiet.
The quiet was where it happened.
The quiet was where the hands moved.
The quiet was where the child learned
that screaming changes nothing.
I could not let the quiet win.
I filled it with questions.
I filled it with proof.
I filled it with my need
to finally
for once
be the one who sees
before the hand falls.

Soon the room filled with explanations
stacked like unsent letters,
like the words I never spoke ,

like the names of the dead
I am still forbidden to mourn.
The walls grew thick with them.
The windows fogged with them.
We breathed explanation
until there was no air left
for love to breathe.

And love
That poor exhausted thing,
poor animal backed into a corner,
poor bird with the broken wing
kept answering.
Kept trying.
Kept pressing its small warm body
against the bars of my ribs.
Kept bringing tea.
Kept staying late.
Kept saying it again:
I am here. I am still here. I am not leaving.

But I did not believe.
I could not believe.
Belief was the first thing they took.
Belief died in the small room.
Belief is buried with the child
who still screams.

Until one evening
it left.
Not with anger.
Not with a slammed door.
Not with the violence I understood,
the violence I was waiting for,
the violence I had already prepared for,
the violence that would finally prove
that I was right all along.

Only the absence
where a body used to be.
Only the space
where tea was once poured.
Only the silence
I had been interrogating
for years
finally answering
with itself.
I killed it.
I stood at the window of my own face
and watched myself kill it.
Question by question.
Proof by proof.
Year by year.
Now the house inside my chest

is very orderly.

Only a chair.
Only the chair.
Only the empty chair
where love once sat
patiently
under interrogation.
Where love once sat
and answered
and answered
and answered
until there was nothing left
to answer with.

And the terrible calm
of questions
that have finally run out of answers.

I sit in the orderly house.
I count the silences like inventory.
I have become very good at counting.
I learned from the people.
I learned from the nights.
I learned from the years
of swallowing the names
of everything I loved

until I loved nothing
and no one
and the house was safe
and empty
and mine.

Sometimes I think I hear footsteps.
Someone approaching .
But it is only the wind.
It is only the past.
It is only the child
still digging in the dark of the chest,
still looking for the door
that was never there,
still believing
that if she is quiet enough,
good enough,
still enough,
someone will come
and explain
why love always leaves.

No one comes.
No one explains.
No one is coming.
But love?
Love came once.

Love sat in the chair.
Love answered every question.
Love stayed until there was nothing left of it
but the echo of its voice
saying I am here
over and over
until here became there
and I became alone
and the chair became empty
and I became the one
who made it empty.

I made it empty.
I, who was emptied first,
learned to empty.
I, who was interrogated,
learned to interrogate.
I, who was questioned,
learned to question
until nothing survived the questions.
Not love.
Not you.
Not me.
Not the child.
Not anyone.

And the child is still digging.

Still screaming.
Still waiting for someone
to explain
why the hands that took
were the only hands
that ever stayed.

I am the one who sits here now,
waiting for a love again
that will never come back
because I asked it
for its papers
one too many times.
I asked it for its papers
and it showed me its heart.
I asked again
and it showed me its hands
empty, open, offering.
I asked again
and it showed me its leaving.

This is how I learned
that love is not patient.
Love is not kind.
Love is a thing that can be exhausted
like the child's last scream
before she learns

that screaming changes nothing.

I exhausted it.
I drank it dry.
I questioned it to death.
I held it under the water of my need
until it stopped moving.
I am the one who killed it.
I am the one who sits here now,
in the orderly house,
in the empty chair,
in the silence I demanded,
finally getting what I asked for.

17. Act Like it

They said keep yourself busy.
I was folding clothes in the bedroom
and the laundry was warm,
and I was cold. Cold from the inside out.
My hands shaking like the last leaves.

Busy yourself, they said again,
and I could hear them in the kitchen,
the clink of forks on plates,
the smell of chicken frying,
the sound of their voices smooth as butter,
and I was trying to survive my own lungs,
each breath a glass of water
I had to drink without spilling,
each breath a knife I had to hold
without cutting myself.

There were marks on my wrists.
Small red sentences I wrote
when no one would listen.
They had a smell, those cuts
metallic, like coins on the tongue,
like licking the inside of an old tin cup.
They stung when the water hit them.

They itched when they healed.

I held out my arms to them, like a beggar.
Like a saint offering wounds
to the unbelievers.
They looked.
I watched their eyes travel down
to the red lines, the scabs,
And they looked away.
I felt their looking away
like a door closing in my face.
I heard it in the silence
that filled the room after.
I tasted it in my mouth
metal again, but older,
like sucking on a penny
from the year I was born.

You're seeking attention, they said,
and their voices were flat,
like stones dropped in water,
like the sound of the refrigerator hum
that never stops, that you forget
until someone points it out
and then you cannot stop hearing it.

Inside my head everything had teeth.

I would wake at three in the morning
and the walls were breathing.
I could hear them, low and slow,
like an animal sleeping in the plaster.
The wall, white with purple stars,
seemed to pulse in the dark.
I would press my ear to it
and hear something moving inside.
Something larger.
Something with a heartbeat.

The furniture rearranged itself
when I was not watching.
I would walk into the living room
and the chair by the window
had turned slightly toward me,
like it had been waiting.
Waiting and watching.
The television, dark and silent,
reflected the room back at itself,
and in its black glass I saw
a girl
a girl who lived inside the television.

They said you're making things up.
They said stop imagining things.
But the things were real.

The things stood at the foot of my bed
wearing my own face.
I could feel them there,
the weight of them on the mattress,
the cold they brought with them,
the smell of old photographs,
of places where light never reaches.
They watched me watch them.
They waited for me to blink first.

I never blinked first.
I learned to sleep with my eyes open.
I learned that the dark has a taste
like dust, like the inside of a closet.

I said something is wrong.
My voice came out small,
a bird with a broken wing,
a thing that could not fly
and could not die
and could only sit there
beating itself against the ground.

They said you are ungrateful.
I could smell the dinner cooking.
Roast chicken. Potatoes.
The smells of Sunday,

of family,
of everything I was supposed to feel
and did not feel.
The smell filled the kitchen
and filled my nose
and I wanted to be sick.
I wanted to open my mouth
and let everything out
the chicken, the potatoes,
the years of swallowing
what I could not say.

I said I cannot breathe inside my own head.
They said others have it worse.
I said I am disappearing.
They said you're right here.
And I was. I was right there.
I could feel my feet on the floor,
the cold tile through my socks.
I could smell the cleaner they used on it,
lemons
And ammonia,
the smell of things being erased.
I could hear the clock in the hallway
ticking like a heart that would not stop.
I was right there.
But I was also somewhere else.

I was under water.
I had always been under water.
The water was cold and dark
and it filled my ears so their voices
came to me bent and strange,
like songs played underwater,
like words spoken through glass.

Then came the verdict.
Difficult.
The word arrived like a stone.
I felt it in my hand.
I felt its weight, its cold,
the way it fit perfectly
in the palm like something
that had always belonged there.
They passed it between them at dinner.
I watched their hands.
I watched the stone move
from mother to father,
father to mother.
I heard it click against their glasses.
I smelled their skin on it,
the lotion my mother used,
the soap my father liked.

Too much.

They said
I woke wearing it.
A shirt I could not take off.
Too tight at the throat.
Too heavy on the shoulders.
Too much meant I took up space.
I could feel myself taking it,
the air around me getting thick,
the room shrinking when I entered.
I could see it in their faces,
the way they pulled back slightly,
the way the air between us
grew longer, colder,
the way they stopped touching me.

Crazy.
Final verdict.
After the white room.
After the pills that made my thoughts
feel borrowed, like wearing a dead girl's coat.
The coat smelled of her.
Some other girl's fear.
Some other girl's mother.
Some other girl's dinner table
where the chicken was always hot
and the words were always stones.
I wore it anyway.

I wore it because my own clothes
had been taken.
I wore it because it was cold
and they said this was the only coat
I would ever need.

You said act normal.
I tried.
But normal tastes like nothing.
Normal is the space between tastes,
the moment when you are hungry
And your tongue is waiting for something
and nothing comes.
I could not find it.
I could only find the other tastes
the metal, the salt, the dust,
the sour of not believing,
the sweet of pretending,
the bitter of swallowing
everything I could not say.

Normal sounds like the hum
of a refrigerator you have forgotten.
The sound that is always there
until it stops,
and then the silence
is louder than anything.

I could not find normal.
I could only find the other sounds
the walls breathing,
the furniture moving,
the television speaking
in its dead electric voice,
the clock ticking like a bomb
I was supposed to disarm
with no instructions.
So I act like it now.
I act like the daughter who finally learned
to wear the skin they sewed for her.
Inside out. The seams showing.
I can feel them against my body,
those seams, those places
where they hurried,
where they ran out of thread
and used my voice instead.
I can feel it pulling when I speak,
the thread they took from my throat,
strand by strand,
while I slept and dreamed
of being heard just once.

I walk through the house.
My feet on the floor.
The cold tile. The warm carpet.

I can smell the dinner cooking.
Chicken again. Always chicken.
The smell fills the kitchen
and I stand in it
and I do not eat.

I pass my mother.
She smells of lotion and coffee.
I pass my father.
He smells of soap and newspaper.
They pass me.
I smell of water.
I smell of the drowning
they never saw.
I smell of the cuts
they never read.
I smell of the crazy
they named me
in the language of fine
and good
and okay
and pass the salt
and what's the weather
and we have everything
and you have everything
and why are you still standing there?
why do you look at us like that?

You are too sensitive
why are you still here
why are you still
why you

I act like it.
Not because I am
what they named me.
But because if I must carry their words
I will carry them well
like a mirror held up
to their own faces.

Do you see me now.
My voice is small.
A bird with a broken wing.
Beating against the ground.

Do you see me now.
My skin is cold.
It smells of water.
It smells of the bottom
of the lake.

Do you see me now.
I am standing right here.
I am always right here.

I am the crack in the mirror
that will not stop looking.
I am the water rising.
I am the storm
they built with their silence,
their weather,
their chicken for dinner,
their looking away.

Do you see me now.
The answer is always
the same smell
coffee and lotion,
soap and newspaper,
chicken burning
on the stove.

The answer is always
the same sound
the clock ticking,
the refrigerator humming,
their voices smooth as butter
discussing the weather
in the next room
while I drown
in this one.

The answer is always
Weather
Chicken
the same taste
metal,
salt,
nothing.

The answer is always
no.

18. Other POV

This is not a house. It is a sea.
You are the drowned woman
who forgot to stop walking.

I find you on the shore each evening,
your lungs full of salt,
your eyes still searching
for the ship that went down
twenty years ago.

You do not know you are wet.
You do not know
the water follows you everywhere,
that I sleep in a tide pool,
that our bed is a reef
where your past tangles
its kelp around my ankles.

I have learned to breathe
in your weather system.
Low pressure always.
The sky that color
before the storm breaks
you wear it like skin.

Some mornings you are clear.
I can see the continent of you,
the architecture of bone,
the ports where love might dock.
By afternoon, the fog rolls in.
Not from outside.
From you.
You exhale it.
You become it.
I reach for you
and my hand comes back
Holding an absence.

Your trauma is not a room.
It is an ocean.
I am not a visitor.
I am a vessel.

I have been small enough
to sail your veins.
Large enough
to carry the weight
of every shipwreck
you keep in your cargo hold.

You do not know

you are carrying them.
You think the dead weight
is just living.
You think everyone
walks with this drag,
this anchor
that catches on nothing
and everything.

When you flinch
from my hand,
I do not see a door closing.
I see a wave
pulling back from shore,
gathering itself
for the violence
it learned
before it knew
it could be still.

When you disappear
into your silences,
I do not see a room
with the lights off.
I see a diver
going down too deep,
lungs burning,

looking for something
She left
at the bottom
of a childhood
that was not her.

You tell me once
about the man.
The one who made you
a seabed
before you knew
what it meant
to be walked on.

You tell me clinically,
like a marine biologist
describing a dead zone
the way oxygen leaves,
the way nothing grows,
the way the water
still looks like water
but cannot hold life.

I listen.
I am listening.
But I am thinking:
This is my lover's mouth

speaking his own murder.
describing the place
where she learned
that love is a current
that takes without asking.

I have become a student of pressure.
The way you hold yourself
like a deep-sea creature
who would explode
if brought too quickly
to the surface.

The way my tenderness
is a kind of drowning to you
too much light,
too much air,
too much of what
you were taught
would kill you.

I calibrate.
I become
the exact temperature
of survival.
Warm enough to feel,
cold enough

not to burn.
I am a thermostat
in the house of your body,
always adjusting,
always failing.

Some nights you surface.
Not all the way
just enough
to see the moon,
just enough
to remember
there is an above.

Those nights,
you hold me
like I am the first air
you have tasted
in years.
You put your mouth
to my throat
as if to drink
the sound of someone
who stayed breathing.

I do not tell you
that I am drowning too.

That loving you
is learning
to live without oxygen.
That my lungs
have become gills,
that I am adapting
to an environment
that was never meant
to hold me.
Your past is a current
I cannot navigate.
It has its own weather,
its own tides,
its own laws
about what sinks
and what floats.

I am not a strong swimmer.
I only know
how to hold on.
How to wrap myself
around you
when the riptide comes.
How to go under
and under
and under
and still

find the surface
with you in my arms.

You ask me once,
in the hour between tides,
when the water is still
and your eyes are clear
as a child's who has never
seen the ocean:

Why do you stay?
I could say:
because I have seen
what lives in your depths
the wreckage,
the bones,
the small light
of a fish
that has never seen the sun
and I am not afraid
of the dark.

I say nothing.
I pull you down
into the sheets
like a tide pulling out.
I hold you

in the place
where water meets air,
where drowning meets breathing,
where you meet me.

Here is the truth
I do not tell you:

I stay because
I have become
a creature of your depths.
My body has changed.
My eyes are large now,
used to the dark.
My skin is cold,
used to the pressure.
My heart beats slow,
used to the waiting.

If I left,
if I surfaced,
I would explode.
The light would kill me.
The air would be too thin.
I would gasp
and gasp
and gasp

for a kind of oxygen
I no longer remember.

So I stay.
Not because you need me.
Not because love is noble.
But because
in the black water of you,
I have found
the only pressure
my bones can bear.

You surface sometimes.
Not for long.
Just long enough
to see my face
in the moonlight,
to wonder
who this man is,
this stranger

I do not say:
I am the one who waited.
I am the one who learned to breathe water.
I am the one who chose
the dark
over the dark without you.

I only touch your face
this drowned woman
who forgot to stop walking,
this ocean
that became a person,
this water
I have learned to call home
and I let you
forget again.
I let you
go back down.
And
I follow.

19. Aftermath

I thought my life was small, a room,
a sealed jar. A few sounds I could almost
keep from breaking. A mouth
I practiced shutting.

No one told me grief
is not a room but a cell
without walls. Once inside,
you forget there was ever a door.
The language of return rots on your tongue.

So I walked.
Over flats of almost
almost held, almost seen,
almost enough to make a person
out of scraps.

The ground gave up its dead.
Each version of me I'd tried to bury
rose with my own face,
hollowed, asking:

What did you flatten
to be held?

What did you sever
to remain?

And the sky
the sky said nothing.
That was its answer.

A silence older than bone
unspooled in my chest:

You built altars from throats
and called it prayer.
When they closed,
you called it god leaving.

I wanted to say
It was hunger.
It was the only shape
I knew how to wear.

But the universe does not hear.
It only empties.

I saw it then
how I knelt
at the altar of any hand,
how I offered myself

like an extra thing,
a thing you set down
and forget.

And still
I was not spared.
Isn't that the true horror?

The collapse was not the end.
The betrayal kept breathing.
The loneliness grew teeth
and learned my name.

Instead
it carved.
It hollowed.
It made a space
that nothing fills.

A version of me
that no longer begs
because begging is a muscle
that has died.

That does not shrink
it was already
pressed flat.

That does not mistake
the wound
for the whole.

So let the world take.
It always takes.

Let it erase my plans,
scorch my illusions,
scatter what was left
like salt thrown on soil.

I am no longer
a fragile thing waiting.

I am the question
that eats itself.

I am the aftermath
that stays aftermath.

And everything I love
has already left.

So.
When the universe speaks

I do not listen.
There is nothing left
to answer with.
Only the place
where a voice
used to be.

20. An open door

I saw you today
moving through the light
like a guest who had misplaced
the key to their own name.

You wore joy like a dress
that did not fit,
and I recognized the hem,
the careful fold,
the way the hands smooth
what the heart cannot.

I wanted to tell you:
it is not failure
to feel the room
before you feel the celebration.

Some of us learn happiness
the way we learn a second language
haltingly,
with an accent that never fully fades,
with words that feel borrowed
until one day
they are not.

That day may not be today.
But today,
you stood in the lantern light,
and I stood with you.
Not to fix.
Not to fill the hollow
with easy answers.
Only to say:
I do not need you to be happy
or me to be glad you are here.

The sugar on your palm
is real.
The arms that held you
did not measure
how much you held back.
The laughter that moved through you
like a current through stone
it left something,
even if you could not name it.

I have learned
that joy does not always arrive
as arrival.
Sometimes it comes
as the space beside you

growing quiet enough
for you to hear your own breath
without apology.

Sometimes it comes
as a hand
that does not ask you
to be anything
other than what you are
even when what you are
is a room
waiting for its door
to open.

Today,
the door did not open.
But it did not close either.
And I think
I think the door
is learning
to recognize your hand.
So let the day be sweet
without demanding sweetness.
Let the light fall
where it falls.

One day,

without warning,
the laughter will not feel borrowed.
The dress will fit.
The room will welcome you
not as a guest
but as the one
who belongs.

Until then,
I will stand beside you
in the courtyard,
not asking you to enter,
only to know:
the festival
is not diminished
by your silence.
And neither
are you.

21. What the Pink Mountains Keep- For my Inner Child

I have been looking for you
in the wrong rooms.
I thought I had to leave you behind
to become someone
who could carry grief.
I thought the door you opened
for every stranger
was the same door
I learned to close.

But you
you painted mountains pink
not because they were pink
but because pink was the sound
your heart made
when it was not afraid.

I remember your hands.
How they held the brush
like it was a hand
you were meeting for the first time.

How you dressed for the morning
as if the day itself
was a stranger
you already loved.
A yellow dress.
A ribbon you tied twice
because once was not enough
for all the happiness
you were bringing.

You met everyone
with your whole face.
You did not know
there was another way to meet.
Kindness was not a choice
it was the air
you breathed
before anyone told you
to hold your breath.

Little one, I need you to know:
I did not mean to lock the door.
I did not mean to fold your red ribbon
into a drawer
and call it growing up.

The summers without sun

they were not your fault.
The altars I built from throats
they were never
what you taught me.

You taught me mountains
can be any color
if you look at them
with your whole chest.
You taught me strangers
are just people
I have not yet painted pink.
You taught me getting ready
is a kind of prayer
the ribbon, the dress,
the small ceremony
of telling the world
I am here
and I am wearing joy
like it has always fit.

I want to dress you again.
I want to tie the ribbon
and let you choose the yellow
even if the day is gray.
I want to stand at the door
with you

and let the stranger in
before fear
learns their name.

I have walked continents
to find you,
only to realize
you were not lost.

You were the pink
I stopped seeing.
You were the kindness
I stopped believing
was still inside me.
You were the hand
that never stopped holding
the brush
I just forgot
to look
at what I was painting.

So let me sit beside you now.
Let me watch you paint
the mountains
whatever color
they need to be.
Let me meet the stranger

at the door
with your open face.

I am not too late.
The ribbon is still red.
The dress is still yellow.
The day is still
a stranger
I can choose
to love.